MW01121279

placeholder

Charmaine Cadeau

Brick Books

Library and Archives Canada Cataloguing in Publication

Cadeau, Charmaine, 1977-
     Placeholder / Charmaine Cadeau.

Poems.
ISBN 978-1-926829-81-4

     I. Title.

PS8605.A34P53 2013   C811˃.6   C2013-900061-5

We acknowledge the Canada Council for the Arts, the Government
of Canada through the Canada Book Fund, and the Ontario Arts
Council for their support of our publishing program.

The author photo was taken by Nathaniel Ward.

This book is set in Minion Pro, designed by Robert Slimbach and
released in 1990 by Adobe Systems.

Design and layout by Cheryl Dipede.
Printed and bound by Sunville Printco Inc.

Brick Books
431 Boler Road, Box 20081
London, Ontario N6K 4G6

www.brickbooks.ca

Contents

Sea legs

Doesn't mean standing where the ocean once
smacked, dirt shells under your feet. In Wisconsin,
jellyfish fossils billow like nighties
turned to emery, another take on Lot's wife. But over here, just sand,
inlaid sand once beach and the feeling of being outlaw, outlier.

Means after being on the water, fluid in the inner ear
copies the boat's aggressive curtseys,
cochlea remembering itself as nautilus. That when back
ashore, the land sways. A nonchalant gravity,
one that threatens to carry you off.

Signal breaking up

Only some of what you're saying gets through,
the rest marionettes, angular joints half
alive. And silence.

Clutch of lupines on the dash, the shade of summer homes:
you're driving through the mountains again, split
rock highways, salt marsh. An ordinary eye,
no chance

of deer. At home, I'm worrying
the dark finish
off the arms of the chair, the part
that curves down.

We're playing, I know we're playing
a game, and if I go
so far as to think about
cheating, deep down I suspect
I've palmed the wrong piece.

I repeat myself again, and again everything falls
helpless into that underwater cotton deafness leaving
only a feeling of needing to come
up for air.

They're everywhere, girls
who know how to whisper the right things, get
through. You can spot a mermaid by the pink
curl of her ear: beachy soft-serve twist, a conch,
a cinch, easy to unwind.

Reveal

Birds spun of the most transparent
sugar-glass flit between us wherever
we go, the warble from their throats
sounding like a verse of couldn'ts.
Couldn't help it.

When you take
hold of one, its heart flashes
apricot and pops like the filament
in a hot light bulb.
All that's left is rattle.

The sky, the room: shut.
Stone-still.
But then remember
moving in that winter,
those months not knowing what would come

up in the garden, coat those unstrained branches.
All we could do was wait for buds, the
leaving.

It could've turned out so differently.

Erosion

We tend toward disintegration like grace
notes, half-apparent, ash becoming

air. Slow loss we can't prevent is the hardest
to grieve. The wedding band wrought to bone

smoothness, colours we chose and can't quite remember
how they gleamed before being

bleached in the living room sunlight. Bluebottle flies
drone as if they've forgotten the words.

One is caught between glass panes.
The small struggle their way into seeing, and we'd

help, if we could. If only the heart had
antennae. If only the heart had antennae to tap

out the way to the safest places, the ones
run by the slowest clocks. Alongside sowbugs

curling in the damp beneath the woodpile.
The chopping block, a blossom of scars.

Below my knee, a thin white stroke
waving like lightning stays numb when touched.

If only tenderness was always so exquisitely roofed
under thickened skin. If only there was room enough to tuck

away our losses instead of having them fall like calendar
days in movies, aspen leaves fluttering at our feet.

Six workdays

Begin with exhalation, somewhere between a runner's pant and a sigh, between a low D held on the clarinet and a sneeze, blowing up balloons and puffing bangs out of your eyes. This breath is the first spread of space where none was before: fine linen unfurled for a picnic, the man on the bus sitting with his knees apart, thighs like a wishbone; the stillness beneath an umbrella. Suspend the world here: a drop of boiling candy set in a glass of cold water. Make the first light: a struck match, a flashing neon sign, the glowing wake of comb jellies and corals.

The water, divide. Curdle some to make clouds that scull across the blue horizon. Set aside some part for slow, low rolling fog. Play with in-between: sleet and thunder, snowflake one-off's shivery needlelace, rainbow's repetitive prisms. Upwards, steam columns and the invisible flight of droplets from a swimmer's skin. Separate sloshing waves, fine spray a pop can makes when you open it, whirlpools and tides, undertow and bubbles. Air should be thick enough to hold in perfumes, slow down the click and flutter of an Asian fan, bead to the skin like a kiss held in space.

Press a rock into the centre like the pea in king's cake or the jade hearts Aztecs set in statues. Fly over cresting waves, sink boulders for sea caves. Skip stones to sink as islands. Part land with rivers to fill the bellies of lakes. Spread mud flats and topsoil, swamps and tar pits. Make quicksand muffle while the desert dunes hum and sing. Shove slabs into mountains, coax clay into memory, toss sand into everything. Sow algae and lawns, vines and twinflowers. Build fine parasols on seeds to carve into wind.

Hang the sun: a yolk is anchored by transparent chalazae. In pearl sheen, wash everything. Close the day with tones of poppies, pink hyacinth. In the black sky, make a snowy moon. String stars like patio lanterns, fragments of broken glass, dust; some unhinge in space, dragons blazing in quick arcs. Planets can be strung like baubles, terrestrials, Jovians. The Milky Way lies like petals afloat in a road puddle, the North Star a root. Northern lights, like genies, smokeless in a harvest sky, fluid as the wishes you release this time of day.

Cup between your palms a grape stalk. Dream it to bone. Flood rivulets, the circulatory system. Stretch heart chambers, twitching muscle, skin. Sculpt gills, combs, scales as jewelled armour, feathers knit by hook and eye. Set fish to tail-stroke in schools, pitch birds like wedding rice. The sailfin and loon slip through surfaces, hover the border. Snug eggs in jelly, nests that honeycomb the cliff face, froth in reeds. Spill intent: dark creeping pools of squid, leech, eel. Design protection: spines, beaks, a crawling train of plated lobsters. Compose for whales, fine-clawed wrens. Clams, sea stars: quiet parts.

Start the day with spiders marking travel lines in webs, hanging with their legs folded. In negative space, place antlers between branches. Thread fur onto hide, thick for bears, dandelion wisps for rabbits. Comb in colour, stripes, dots. Tuck among stalactites, bats. Fill forests with yips, snorts, a stampede of hoofs and claws. Weave skin that's bare, camouflaged, toxic, blushing. Underground moles, dug worms. Scatter flocks of gnats, pinch dragonflies to toss as darts. Nestle mice and foxes in holes. Shell centipedes, snails, and turtles, whatever's left to make.

What remains is rest: the trick of seasons and perennial flower beds, silence and deferring. Make a soft lampshade, the glow of a chrysalis; fallow fields and drought. Place in weekend retreats and long bus trips, chamomile and yawning. Let the body ache so much you can't remember falling asleep.

Moonish eyes, w tchful. The sharpest beak plucking our pr mise, a familiar mouse.

And still we hold tight to longitude, a diarist's ambition. Someday we'll buy a cottage, hammer out our b at, sailing.

S ng in the bulrushes, l ve wire: the electric troubadour sn p. Crickets, their constancy.

M st of the morning lying on the grass.

We'll always burst from the paddock, f lly-hearted, that brimming error, multiply our m ths, what we vanquished and brought home, dusty wings knocking the lampshade.

Always come back to that kiss, the tongue a lock and each, in turn, l cksmith.

M nish yes, w tchful. The sharpest b k plucking our pr mise, a f miliar m se.

And st ll we hold tight to long t d , a diarist's ambition. S med y we'll buy a cott g , h mmer out our b at, s il ng.

S ng in the bulr shes, l ve w re: the electric tr bad r sn p. Crickets, the r constancy.

M st of the morning lying on the grass.

W 'll always burst from the paddock, f ll -h arted, that brimming err r, multiply r m ths, what we vanquished and brought home, dusty wings kn king the l mpshade.

Always c me back to that kiss, the tongue l ck and   ch, n t rn,
l cksm th.

Mo n sh yes, w tchful. The sh rpest b   k pl cking   r pr m se,
   f m l r mo se.

And st ll we h ld t ght t long t d , a di rist's ambit n. S m d y
we'll b y a cott g , h mm r out our b at, s l ng.

S ng n the b lr shes, l ve w re: the l ctric tr   bad   r sn p. Cr ck ts,
th r c nst ncy.

M st f the morning lying n the gr ss.

W 'll lways burst from th p ddock, f ll -h art d, th t brimming
   rr r, m ltiply   r m ths, what we v nqu shed and bro ght h me,
d sty wings kno king the l mpsh d .

   lw ys c me b ck to that k ss, th tong   l ck and   ch, n t rn,
l cksm th.

Attendant spirits

Winter thirst, confetti snow. The only way out is to dig.
What was that you said about fossils, spoked crinoids?
Make-believe stars, ship's wheels, compass roses.
And every one's unique.

These still months,
the static cling, reminding yourself it takes
longer to get anywhere. Light comes from the ground,
a cold, reflective flame.

In a week, we'll cut a tree and the house
will smell like outside: that memory of carding wool.
Sweat and stone fences.

Children on the lake skate around
the white blisters in its surface
thin enough to catch a blade, send someone headlong.
A boy's scarf is tied over his eyes to draw teams, hockey sticks
piled in the middle of their circle like bonfire tinder.

I want it to be because of the sun this time of year,
how we're positioned in space, that I can't
stop thinking about a room so dark you can't find the body.
And below the ice, the pull.

Queen bee

I dream about her, poised deep in her hive,
hollow and light as echo. Larvae
stretch to hinges and fuzz, commas anticipating the next
ink string. The wax lattice hugs
pollen from a thousand orchard flowers.
Broad comb the color of blood oranges, while the apiary

glows like polished oak. She's the Wizard
of Oz behind the curtain,
all levers and smoke. She's pipe cleaners, rubber band
whir, the laundry lint in my blue jeans pocket. Sometimes she seems
enchanted like a daffodil that sprang to flight when kissed, a toy from
somewhere they're still made by hand. One that bites. Her body's

made of snow, you can tell by how she hovers, shakes. Inside
the nest, her cell's a freckle, a typo,
a neighbourhood yard no one cuts across, the photograph
missing from an album. She's both anchor and wing, the sheet
strung in the spring river to rinse. Raindrops clinging to
windshield glass, the

structure of her eyes through which
everything's a swarm, pieces held by little more than force of
habit. The way it feels to cross a crowd,
need looking after, carry a gun
strapped to your leg. She's Saturn, surrounded by
a hexagonal cloud, dust and ice rings, shrapnel

satellites—an exploded planet. Close up
her cell's architecture is the same as steroids, cholesterol,
graphite lines ghosting up through watercolours, aspirin
loose in the desk drawer, a crystal chandelier, the scutes of
a painted turtle's shell, a
swerve of stripes. She's always coming up sixes,

doing the polka, counting the beats.
She's the friend I forget to call, a stout heart.
She wants to get away from here.
She retracts like honey
dissolving on the tongue. A silent partner.
The workers hum and build like canary

girls in a munitions factory—skin yellowing from TNT. They
think about demolition,
what the last sound would be, the catch—

Operator

Doggedly, you've tried to get through and she,
being pure astral body,
left you alone with your voice.

Held, as though between rooms.
The body's confusion between falling
and falling asleep. An old nerve.

The distant switchboard, atmosphere
of zeros, clean white
plates. Ghosts on the other end:
dull tones of tires on pavement,
highway speeds.

Dialing the number again, seven
wives for seven brothers. The fist-sized
birds, the stone: it's all in the wrist, flicking
between when to hold out, when to let go.

Blueprint

We're in a house made of light.
Door latches click like eyelids
blinking, like breaking
open an orange.

Walking through
rooms we feel not like twin yellow-eyed cats
lolling in a window but their fur,
indiscreet and warm.

Our kitchen's fashioned after the barn that blazed.
Everything sleeping. A glow on
autumn cornfields that should have been the sun
rising. Shadows in the corner of the bedroom

assemble into a closet, strangle sweaters and extra
hooks, and on the ceiling, faint
waves like what you'd see
if you were at the bottom of a cold lake

looking toward the surface. Down the hallway, an iridescent
glimmer leans in as if someone's
left a television on, or maybe it's the aquarium, angel-
fish patrolling back and forth. The den's palette

was hard to get right, that lived-in look. For the walls,
we mixed noonday tangled in leafy
branches with the cloudlessness of a display
case, one that shows off doll-white hands and necks.

Carpets spark like camera flashes
under each step, like summer lightning,
the electric smell of prairie grass, shorted wires.
In this house we drift

like asteroids flicked along by sunrays,
dust motes before they settle. We say little,
taking our cues from embers, bright piths
feathered with ashes, wearing down.

Weatherproof

Close your eyes. The first day of winter,
smoke knitted to wool and leaning at the hip
a cord of wood creaking out the last of its green.
Snow ash wheeling, book pages
born into moths, a hungry alphabet.

Against the frosted glass,
press your hand.
Brittle grass heaves in places, a sleeping
flock of geese, the field all
pencil lines, here and here
smudged.

Watch the shifting of an empty room
as you enter—or, from your lungs
blow out the perfect
door, white against the house—

The way it really begins.
On the windowsill, seven dead bees,
wings tied prettily back: fists of air
hardened off.

Hide-and-seek

We dance, we dance
        like the flick and strut of dust on a film reel,

wingbeats of killdeer pulling away from stonebed
        nest. We hum and sing, topping marmalade jars

with burlap circles and bows. We mouth muggy
        greenhouse words that sprout vegetables in the fat air

between us. We burst in godly style from seafoam, fasten
        sequins to our clothes. We tuck away, seam

keepsakes in the squint of a beetle's elytra. We build and
        wait, a pair of shoes slung up on the telephone line,

and seek the shut-ins and disappeared, loose
        floorboards, clams blowing

nostrils in the beach sand, and have-you-seen
        faces on the lamppost by the house. Strands

of the photographer's hair blown in front of the lens
        are lines of absence, magic wands,

caught as this picture is snapped.

Side effects

Walk this steep road turning
sharp around the guardrailed river, dust
tamped under a coat of Dombind.
Settle for a minute as if the body's
pooled like the weight of cool air,
pulled to dogtooth violet, log driver
bruising as he slipped a hundred years
ago: swift timber his last sky.

As if the whipped backstitch of sparrows
sews you in, and as if you could cut through,
the glint of scissors signalling from your fingers,
the descending glow of tin punch lanterns
once left along the banks,
fish scales on a knife, campfire sparks swinging
out of smoke.

On a branch overhead
beak-divots map constellations where ants curl
under the surface. As if anything could be safely
sealed away. Wildflower seeds
pocket themselves sinking through moss and
creepers into larval sleep: more of that afternoon
nap. A landscape of lean-tos and parasitic
puddles.

As if everything helps itself,
helplessly. Guided by bread crumbs, the
flannel of porch light.

Imposters

An object encounters its image, an object encounters its name.
It may be that the image and the name of the object encounter
each other.

—René Magritte, "Words and Images"

JOHN DOE:

I don't feel quite like myself today.

JANE DOE:

What's in a name.

A beat

Glasshouse

We like the idea of plain glass in our first house: bowls, apothecary jars, bottles on mantles or sills. We catch ourselves wondering if all this emptiness will make us feel hungry, or in such a way we can't put a finger on, the word for it tasteless, a dead nerve. Since glass is sand, can we call this place our beach home? We wonder what our neighbours would think if our walls were see-through, too, would we be too boring to watch? Could we harbour any illusions. We can't cast stones, but maybe rip open feather pillows, the down clinging to our hair like movie snow. We talk about who will dust the glass, will we take turns, brighten it with vinegar, would we ever put anything inside: newsstand flowers, waxed fruit, warped bottle caps picked up while walking the dog? And who will collect these things anyway, and will we get a dog. And if the dog smells up the house at least the glass is odourless. We wonder if you can really shatter glass by screaming, a perfect treble, or is that only for crystal? And if in this way one of us or the dog with knobby legs breaks any glass, what then? Turn out all the lights, point a flashlight at the floor to pick up what winks back. And know for years to come because of what we won't see, spaces we can't reach, shards from this day will plant themselves under the pads of our feet, make those keen blood-blooms. As always with glass, the threat of upset, and seeming irreplaceable still.

Word problem

A perfect body rolls. The sum of its parts.
Us, on separate trains, the point we touch.

Finding the value of k. Kimono. Kangaroo mouse.

Using stragmatics to determine how many times
he'll pass before half the lawn is mowed.

Not getting exactly what you put into it, i.e., this + this = that;
e.g., the marriage equation.

Size of the shaded part. Unequal rows.
The length of the ladder, degrees from the wall,
odds of having bad luck if you cross beneath it.

What coins she's likely to have. The sides they'll show when tossed.
Velocity of the flip.

Before the dog overtakes the rabbit, count the leaps.
The distance between the hands on the kitchen clock at that moment.

An odd number, three digits, all different, total twelve. The difference
between the first two is the same as the difference between the last.

Independent of the circumstances, having an answer. A set of outputs
for which the problem returns *yes*.

Renters

In all this time, you say, in all
this. And I want to fling

open windows painted shut,
charm your second-hand
jeans into forgetting
the shape of someone
else's body.

The apartment floor's camber: breastbone,
wishbone. A just-so slope, that backstairs
force that leads the body to sleep.

We see the same things.
Cloud acrylic, bare picture hooks.
The water stain on the ceiling tile,
an airship.

Our street's melting: park oaks
curve through icicle glass, always
springtime. On the lawn, toys left overnight
pop like dirty blossoms.

We're nocturnal, after all.
Overcast days, mud-grey mirrors, we shut ourselves
in like a top that when spun
opens its fist, is all bright tin petals.

Wrenches

The city burns, the storm unfastens
everyone. No talk of mercy.

Your men have mutinied. The skiff
won't hold. Damselflies rock above the bay,
wings the watery skin they were born through.

Inoculated against touch, shorelines
hover, silhouettes on the scrim. Blue
hills seen only certain
days churn on the horizon, shadows
nesting in snow: known for giving the slip. How

your fingertips can feel what isn't there. Standing
between trees so tall all that's left is listening:
what sounds like hermit thrush song—half
playground swing, half that trick with a champagne
flute, running a finger around the lilting
rim, the gate home closing tight.

When your family sees you, they'll try to explain.
After the break-in, something always felt
out of place. Detonating like a swarm of sewing
pins dropped to the floor,
impact point traceable but never
all the silver bodies.

The way your face has changed.

Knots, hitches, and bends

The edges advance even now,
a test of balance.

We knew to count glasses of wine those
nights we slept on the cliff last
summer: stars falling.

Rocks and harbour seals pitched below.

How easy it would be to get blown off.
To be pushed, to push: like a tooth

knocked loose, or holding your innards,
trying to fold them back into place.

Forgive the usual for its poise.

Osteology

(Don't) recognize the body for what it is, the wooded
grave. Shy whiteness like mayapple blossoms.
Instead of femur think root, ledge.

Calcite strands arc into cracked ribs,
arrows dropped from a quiver. Blue
legs of storks circle paper umbrellas. Tomorrow

grows out of rock in a nightly pubescent
ache. Call it vertigo, that phantom hurt
of chipped tooth, rheumatic longing, the memory

you had once fallen, been
dragged along the gravel road. Anaesthetic
brooks the clang of funny bone, teeth

colliding in a kiss, the film of skin that slips
across throats of the dead, that grows along
with fingernails and hair. All life

is from life, the invisible nests still
set in winter trees, the hummingbird's
shingled with lichens. Try to accept vanishment,

that a dead spider folded inward becomes
translucent as web, atmosphere. A quick hand,
all fever dream, tucks bright coins

where we lay our heads, close our eyes.
But still, left here, the bones.

Twice as likely

Because meteors cast off wishes as they flash and rattle overhead, because tea leaves still script your secrets in the bottom of the cup, because ESPers and mind-sharing twins make the rest of us feel left out, because love instigates an average number of children and an average rate of divorce, a plainclothes fortune teller works as a statistician. She adjusts the numbers accordingly.

She sees tomorrow as a tease hiking up its skirt at today's loneliness. She sees the days ahead in a tangle of intestines, a shining mirage. The future is flagrant, revealing itself in quartz and moonstone, laundry basins and stainless steel. Try not to look. The future dreams its way onto billboards, makes thatches of branches on our palms, resides in question marks.

What can you take at its word? The gypsy with prophetic dreams and a government job, this future brimming with oracles stuffed in desktops, someone waiting for an answer. Here it is: we're all destined to defeat. Here it is: you're twice as likely to split the bill over cheeseburgers than bœuf bourguignon, you're eighty-nine percent more likely to pick up a penny than pass it by, and one in four dreams of being famous. Here it is: you do it for breathlessness and goosebumps, getting mail and remembering the steps, hearing whale song and the dawn yaps of thrushes echoing from hollow, skyglow chests.

Smugglers

Thick snow-blankets fall intact from March
roofs: that sound of being
carried off.

Keeling clear over
star-drenched shoals, garnet
spindrift in the wake
clinks, ice cubes in goblets, a xylophone
laugh.

Her far-flung love, more skipping
stone than net.

The Great Lake's scent
wreaths her hair,
a mix of algae and the doily
scales of northern pike.

Pulled out flag-long, a knotted
stern line measures speed. The ship,
a garter, a rum-runner's

secret. Fog unravels the horizon, the dirty glass
bottle's lungful of soft
white mould.
As though hesitation had this webbed body.

Drunk: ardour for mischief. Desire
always stumbles, the tilting
deck.

Cutting the engine, pelt-slick
rubber boots step overboard,
bourbon's old heat
gummed molasses-like in the mouth.
Waders scrape the boat

ashore. Then dousing the
bowline with buckets of water to quiet
rope's ache.

Just squelching feet, rushes.

Slip

When someone says Old Timer's instead of Alzheimer's I
keep the correction dangling with the uvula at the back of
my throat because the first thing I noticed when he started
to slip was something we all do, when the word at the tip of
your tongue comes out like whoop-de-doo or jiggerypoke, or
even something more Freudian, calling water wine, or asking
your date if his biological cock is ticking. Then sometimes
our words don't come out at all, hunched like dust bunnies
in our mouths. I'm no armchair psychiatrist but I do believe
in wish fulfillment: he'd call me a stranger's name; we'd hang
on to lucid moments. I think about him aboard the ships he
worked on those years ago, looking ahead to the harbour to
see the faces and figures waving him home, knowing one is
wife but not which one, through the haze.

Keep to yourself

Draw closed the seine over
        silver dashes, sleek impulses, water slipping through
                cupped hands.

       What's been lost
              quietly resurrects in cursive letters, the hammock of
the lowercase *r*, the question mark an ear tuned
for the bolt's slide from inside.

              Carve pages
from a book to put what matters between the covers. And sling
        the rest in the t-shirt you're wearing,
             overflow of apples harvested for a pie
bulging out like zeros.

Some part prefers the dark, presses up in a locket,
                  would change in the telling.

Fusion

Solid, and hard candy
melts to the back seat's upholstery, Alice
slips through the silver
mirror. October sugar maples swoon
as a monarch whips tornados,
orange as nebular bursts of hydrogen,
a leak of rust—
butterfly wings and octopus beaks
both made of chitin.

There are lines we cross, outfitted with liquid
body armour and the knowledge that bones fuse,
that you should swim slowly in quicksand, a lesson
learned from watching grain by grain
backslide in an hourglass.

Everything, a chain of knots, snarls: back
muscles, the home computer wires, the quiet
rip of thin white roots tangled in seeding
pots as they're separated for the garden.

Hard, and yet we take each other in, exchange
breath across our tongues, are closer to rapids than rocks,
more like rain and snowspouts, steam and
fog, seventy percent water, the edges unclear.

What was said

Maybe to understand this story, you'd have to know something about my brother like that he's stoic but unpredictable so when I was in the kitchen washing dishes and we were talking on the phone and I asked if he's going to tie the knot, he said after the restaurant they were standing in snow turning to slop on the street, ring hot in his mitt, and I say, 'So?' Not in a *so-what* sort of way but more like how a champagne cork pops. As he mumbled on, I pictured him rocketing off the ground, alley-ooping in a ninja-meets-superhero version of how he thought he'd grow up when we were young enough to play on the wood floor and not notice how hard it was. Then he said it again, louder for me to catch his drift, 'So she left.' She left.

Whole while

While whole, all along there's been a magnetic
ache for what's left behind in morning
dream, the snapped thread weightless, carried
off. And what's been shucked. Nearly evolved
out of our bones, the part fetching after
forgotten things, birthdays,
a quart of milk, your favourite dirty punchline.

While away a whole afternoon, languid, and the bath steam
curling the paperback. A fleck of pulp—
booklouse, having grown an appetite for words,
skitters to another page. Conjure what to do if
the bridge is out, the epidemic decision to close yourself
off, shelter. See all the empty chairs.

While away, anxieties pile up at the door. Circulars,
the purple nettled lawn.

And that whole while you'd given up, who was looking
after you?

Hole dug, then covered with woven
downed branches. Something falls to the bottom.
Then falls again, this time for the wile
of chasing its own tail, 'long gone' feral twins.
In the mind, a switch flips because we invent necessary company.
Circling again, alone in the trapping pit, wolfish.

Lullaby

Mama says draw the curtains, knees
together. You both know Peeping

Tom's out tonight, sweating at the window,
burrs stuck in his hair real good.

Double dutch girls jump jump
in places you've never been,

behind thistle brush,
in the fairground on a school night.

Sluts in drugstore perfume
conjure up shadow urges

you want to lace tight. Your skin
crawls with winter's breath

that bristles in your shirtsleeves
even after you enter the warm

house. Sit up straight,
Mama says, holding her spoon

and the barred owl on the fence crying
who cooks for you? Who cooks

for you all? Driving here
in the dark from the highway

you can see the sour sky
hugging down on everyone.

How we reminisce

At the table, we split
a red pear, scarred where skin touched
branch, a long-felt hurt.

Another story: small
hum of orchard flies, sweet
juice.

Other people

Other people's children are best taken with their snarly hair and flouncing thank-yous and grimy hands jammed in grimy pockets. Give a half smile for a round of peekaboo, the story about what happened next with grandma, her cheeks like soggy tea bags, and how many words rhyme with blue. If you too have children, your very own set of other people, take other other people's children gladly into your home on school vacation days, the summer months when you start to run out of ideas. They'll dig holes, chase each other, eat savagely. And if you're raising other people's people, not blood relations, all the same rules apply. Buck against the old joke that mothers smother and tame a swatch of space for you alone: they may have been raised by wolves after all, and how are you to know.

Reading ahead to see how it ends

Shoved in kitchen cupboards jars of
dim brine, buttons, and tea leaves
wait—heavy cocoons dreaming ways out.
This witch doesn't keep lures like
apples, candy, a penny too light
for the wish it promises. Back

at home, the future reflects back
in bowls, spoons, the sleekness of
clockfaces. In the lake, tucked light
as a straw, she floats, leaves
spasming above her, face-up and
trying not to read ahead, out

herself. Clouds bloom, dye seeping out
in laundry water. Against her back,
tangling her legs is something like
what she imagines intuition's made of:
sedge and rushes, bass weed leaves
distorted by the surface, their light

feline sweep, fur against calf. Light
pods sway, ready to break out,
sinuous. She's drawn to what leaves
nothing behind: lilies can't go back
once they explode—fragrant stars of
skies spilled, a wild language, like

small knots netting the throat, like
after-effects of blindfolded kisses or light
warning strokes across the soles of
her feet as they slip out
from under her. She thinks back
to how the old story leaves

off, the mewling woman Gretel leaves
blackening in the oven becoming like
fingerprints on glass, oily creosote, back
to seeing her own death: firelight,
the skin of rope stretching out,
skewed pine shadows, the mother-of-

pearl dusk. The waiting crowd shifts,
a heap of stones settling into
relief, everything in its place.

Overexposure

Our photographs came back white, or mostly
white like froth, traces of something else
pressing from the other side.
Holsteins crossing a fog-soaked
road. The blueness of veins.

Swept away, we'd packed for the mountains.
Eclipsed by granite pleats,
we pointed our cameras at ebbing snow,
tide line of lilies in the fray.
The avalanche to come, ghost hooves
hammerstrong over the cliff.

We both as city kids built curbside igloos,
sank into their hollow
hushabye centers and imagined being buried
alive: sled dogs and smoke signals the only way out.

Our pictures now: a hypothermic jive,
throwing off the fur-lined parkas, a troop of roofing nails
sparking at our elbows.
Looking through hot, crooked light,
the open door, fever in my cheeks.

Bounce back

: always comes around again.
Months of playing the shell game: learning to disappear in plain sight.

Because fine linen frays beyond a fix, threads a series of minus signs.
Each line where lips press together, mum.

A night spent rocking, sleep the mirror's deflection on the adjacent wall.
Pearly blink of gills.

The story swims in your blood. And it washes up, no matter how far the toss.

Rest assured, the chimney's the last part standing. That and a lilac
bush beside where the dooryard must have been.

[Few boxes]

Randy's friends have a hard time knowing when to say when, you can't be Randy's friend otherwise. When he decided to move cross-country, he called over everyone he knew. [He wanted us to buy what he wouldn't take with him.] He loudly introduced guests as they walked through the front door, his annunciation having the effect of seeing your name in calligraphy for the first time. The theme was five 'n' dime, all the girls in little black dresses vying to be Holly Golightly. [I wore a gray felt hat to spruce up work-regulation dungarees.] There were stacks of books, pages marked with whatever he was closest to when reading. [A lollipop stick chewed to stalagmite. A deli counter number.] There was a skirmish over the pen with a gorilla on top for the trick it could do. [Randy and I once watched four versions of King Kong in one sitting.] It was hardest to find someone to take the cat, the scruff of its neck always clumped like eyelashes fresh from crying. [The more we wanted to buy things, the less willing he was to sell them.] There was no wine or beer, just back-of-the-cupboard Kool-Aid. [The other theme was potluck.] What I wanted to buy in the end wasn't for sale. The day of Randy's move, we meant to go out for breakfast. [He repacked instead, leaving another few boxes behind.] We met in front of his house with coffee in styrofoam take-out cups. [Whenever I say 'met' I want to replace it with 'meant' the way we do.] We meant with coffee cups, and I stood on the walkway waving until he drove out of sight.

Outlook

Kids play follow-the-leader
under Georgian Bay white pines,
branches windswept to one side like iron
filings pulled by a lodestone.

Air tastes of granite. The last
patch of snow in the grass,
a christening gown—that kind of lace. We
expect the same of the islands: sympathetic
rock will melt into the Huron,
a reflective mass of nerves.

The world is flat. Or, changing degree requires luck,
a sleeveful of larks that gush skyward. The glazed
lake, a spoon's tarnished gut
turning everything upside down.

Dog star

1.

Threadbare sky.
Blindfold knotted
to its mane, the retired
mining mule hoofs
alongside a tall man.

Rolling a square flock of bedsheet
soft from years of washing,
he pushed the needle through
over and again where its wet
eyes would go. Moth holes
for this dazing light.

A mind turns, hipless
sweetgrass undulating.

Will you come home?
The question, now as always.

2.

Tenderness of the quick
reminds us that something's
left from before.

The way weeds
close in on the coal mine
entrance, a vegetable logic.

The way hair
returns to its natural
part.

3.

The saltbox house,
tilting gulls. Chalk line
curtseys on the brink of being
rubbed out.

Indoors, there's shelter. Seeds
tight under pine cone
shingles gradually letting go.

On the beach, pick up
an urchin ring, chiffon bone
china to put where?

4.

The sorrel mule burns at the man's heels,
follows closely as though expecting the edge,
depth under every footfall. The femur's
torque in its socket.

The homonym cleaving: a confusion of devotion
and detachment.

Used to cargo, the mule flexes still. The new lightness
a tailwind, like
slicing through the Achilles
tendon, the slack mess
left without tension on the line.

He finds he repeats himself.
There, there.

5.

Sedative August days.

The slow rumble of glass
lutz marbles
over uneven hardwood floors,
how draggingly
planes pass overhead,
us against the perfect
meadow square,
sheet of pink flowers, knotgrass.

At the story's beginning
everyone's forlorn.

6.

Different sizes,
quick bottles
line the kitchen sill. Bald roots
swell from a trick of light
and water.

Put away leftovers,
scour the sink,
rust growing out of pockmarks,
swash of suds down the drain.

The heart is a footed teacup.
Two birds perching.

7.

The mineral recollection isn't enough;
libertine dust boas
ruffling at the feet.
Woodsmoke
the colour of old lilacs
also in every breath.

Coal dark irises. The sun's a bright penny.

Everything looks the same.
Through the punctured blindfold, infinite white stars.
A handful of round
blossoms left on the fence.

8.

That feeling of being lost.
The subsequent drudge
of stomaching there's no there there.

We all fall short. And still desire,
part and parcel.

9.

Tripping up stairs we taste the dark
and it's hard to find the lamp
switch, the cant of a waking mind
fumbling after its last
dream, a linty kind of light.

Eventually,
eventually the blindfold comes off.

Oh

Nothing surprises so much as your stalking
entrance, cupping your empty hands over my eyes, soft,
soft. Not every day's fit for parades

or travelling amusement parks, you say. No,
today is for ordinary lovemaking. Crouching over
blueberries along the highway, coming

clean. Today, you say, is ripe for returning
to the shipyard for retired boats,
each of them named after a woman, perhaps.

Hope, that's one, and we climb
aboard. But I think we're too heavy, and I'm right, our mouths
on her vowel, feet through the planks, and oh, as we

go down, you blowing dreams like bubbles, me like fine smoke.

Remainder

Trace forensics of time spent apart: road salt from the side of the car
sticks to your jacket, tells where you've been. Foreignness in you, molecular. Antigenic.

The porch step is cleared of snow by the heat of the house. For the first few minutes, I
don't look at your face as though this might send you reeling back. The down
of the neck perked, the open front door.

On the shortest day of the year, take it all in. The sown crop's coarse hide, ceramic
puddles of meltwater. In the cornfield, tender hoofs, hay-reeking piss, the cows broken
out again.

Waking this morning, books fill half the bed, weights and measures, anchorite. Waits,
measures lowland sun-washed against rough beige wool. And who will be the last one
standing?

Secrets

The way to cheat blindfolded. Where you really get it from,
hooking us all in.

      Your workarounds. What won't be passed along.

Her last words, a weapon, a lacy
thatch. How long to let it simmer.

      Holding a letter up to the light
      as if there should be more to the story.

How to cast, clear line spinning
off the reel, sounding like girls whispering, small claws
on hard-packed banks, turning the kaleidoscope, quake of barley,
long-haired hulls.

      Knowing what happens in Bancroft,
      stays in Bancroft. When to say when, who to turn to
      or turn into when the jig is up.

Where the camera's hiding,
how to detect secretions, find a shortcut.
Where to sidestep the overgrown well.

      The actor's under the trap door
      waiting for his cue, heartbeat in the stage boards.

Doorknob to thread to tooth, the overlooked snag,
a tug-of-war, whipsaw rocked by two bodies through ring after ring
mouth-breathing until all they can taste is the fine yellow dust.

      A rabbit's warren, the twisting hollows of a ghost tree's roots.

Where the anchor lay, that kind of cavity. A home for the heart.

I read that mother pelicans kill their young,
bring them back to life with their own blood. That a fish
swallowed the woman's pearl but she was still desirable to the king,
blowing yolk out of the most eggs, the pearl as light as one
hollowed shell.

> The millipede tumbling out of the damp bath towel, pussy-willow
> opacity at the center of ice cubes: we keep these things in the safe.

Carries

North woods at dawn, tawny candlelit
sheen and hesitating lake mist carry off chains,
tufted. The last owl, an aubade. Afterlife.

Blackflies frenzy, boil at the scalp.
Echoing rocks, old company. What happened,
happened.

Days of portaging, the blisters, gray burdocks
crumbling to hundreds of hooks, muscles arrogant
against the weight. Against the slice of shore, freshwater shells,
a blown nest, sprain of mosses and bone.

Each step softer than you'd expect. An improbable
balancing act, shouldering the canoe, the occasional tip, a trail:

compass at the ready, pine needles pointing every which way.

Inside out

Heat comes through smart
girls wearing lipstick
gesturing quotation marks with their fingers.
They're herky-jerky like a dancing
bevy in a silent film, the dark
city dirtying their awkward
dresses. Store windows reflect slick
bodies filled in by anything.

There's no cold light of day, only
the mall's shatterproof sky.
Flecked and flickering,
sparrows wad up nests from burger wrappers,
soft receipts tumbled off of trays—molecular
plastic a near wild glare—and hoist themselves in
atrium trees.

We breathe in perfumes, food-court pretzels,
sweet tobacco from the cigar shop. Exhale,
every cell emptying itself, these small purses.

Two can play

The only game in town, our game's afoot. Roll
up your sleeves to see who rolls with the punches, down for the count,
counting down while the little ones dart, hide
so tough it bends the pin for the dizzy tacker of tails. Heads,
toss the odd man out, a penalty for travelling back to square one.
I might sit this one out. The object's to stay in,
be it, beat it, the clock counting down
snakes and up ladders. Or was it shoots,
the gun in the observatory, Ms. Scarlet dressed as Lady
Luck rooting for the underdog, double-dog daring
while low-blowing smoke at the dice. They're loaded, too.
Dodge that bullet, put a hustle on, the two-sided coin flip, card up
your sleeve, ace in the hole. A shady deal, who's on deck?
No matter who wins, it's how you play. Like a good sport, spit-shake,
carry the day, the trophy, shiningly.

Heard

Everything sings back, the theory of echolocation: that the herd
follows the first to swerve, a melody caught in the ear.

Midday, a slate-blue heron. Wing tips
bolted herringbone tight, its flight a paper doll chain extending and
collapsing. The swinging screen door of the backlot trailer.

I take down the laundry, sailfists in shirtsleeves.
Against my leg, belt-strung keys dream
door after door.

And the thick paint of the shadeless deck sticky underfoot.

Rag of field. Barn beams wither to dirt
and so on. The creeping lives of rust, lichens, their willowy
vibrato.

Wind up

River town, merchants. Canal boats loaded with peat, those fires a stinging homecoming. In the walled city, palm held, Descartes' daughter died of scarlet fever.

Everything comprises its own undoing, proven by the termite's jaw set to self-destruct, autothysis.

He builds a life-sized automaton, gives it her name. Metal wings on her back, a clouded yellow butterfly. Brings her with him to cross the Holland Sea.

Raindrops flatten to parachutes mid-air.

He must have been one of those friends we all have, the sort of whom we say 'that could happen only to him.'

During a storm, the ship's captain, frightened, pushed her overboard. As though inevitable, her small body made up of escapements, bolts, springs.

Sandpipers wheeling in the chest, a filigreed wave.

Sunken, only the sound of needing to be held, a chattering clock. Small buds, barnacles, spreading over her body.

Like riding a bicycle

Remember to lock the door, steady your hand-
le bars, check for Audubon's string tied to the leg.

The sky's a posy of forget-
me-nots. You're driven by whatever turns your crank-
arms.

Every spoke-
n word a bookend.

Worrying over mnemonics, pneumonia, feeling right as rain-
checks. Chap-
eau!

On your bike, grit tosses beneath you, chain-
rings rotating like disc harrows, clapperclaw pin-
wheels a country dentist thought up.

Roving green hillocks, hiccups of turf and mud up-
spring to life as frogs. The oldest muscle-
memory, reflex.

Bridge to the break-
away as you shove to the front of your mind things you don't need to write down:

what possessed you, what makes you shake your head-
set.

Repeat after me: you have an elephant's memory, but in the long run, the hippo-
campus is your ticket home.

Hanging in the air, cotton-
wood seeds reflect dusk like windows covered with sheers. And in the last sun-
lit wedges, gnats held too with celestial gravity. Everything spinning in place.

Possibilities

The fickleness of and/or, a revolving door.

Putting off. Off-putting. The wreak of war.

Afterlife, nightlight. A loose cord.

Flyblown: un-becoming. Cadaver dogs and metaphor.

The saurian

Once, along the greenstone belt, two young friends leapt over
trailing arbutus, bloodroot. Early signs of spring, the cuffed
northern snow. Roget was quick-tempered, a wisp, the bones
of his body appellant. On the other hand, his friend was
contemplative, saying very little, mouthing mostly bedrock.
Whenever Roget would blithely ask his friend to follow him,
he would icily breathe back, 'You mean supervene.' In fact,
his friend often made slight corrections until the boy, feeling
he could never get anything right, stopped coming around,
the conditions for their friendship failing, their stomping
grounds becoming once again overgrown. There was no
word for what had happened, what either felt. Years later,
understanding their estrangement ensued when too many
things were lost in translation, he wrote a book, each line
a monument to compatibility, synonym after synonym, his
dedication in the title and design, covered in moss-plated
scales.

Throwaways

A girl washed up, the body of a girl, and we
set sail until oily in the sun, salt-whipped
hair heavy as ropes.

Dropping anchor, we dove into the sea.
Flecks suspended beneath the surface of an old mirror.
Satellites drifting.

At the heart of that familiar dream
your claw-first body stalls,
destination stretching further away.

Aboard over dinner, we'll only talk
about the warning given to tourists:
throw nothing overboard. How otherwise
a woman can spin anything, the heel
of a bone, into a skyboat, cast off.
Will drown if caught over the ocean when
the yolky sun splits against the horizon,
coracle turning back to a thin shard.

Shades

These ghosts wait. Small
movements hardly count,
like turning the vase so
sunlight nudges more deeply
between petals. No one
really notices, more like how

a watch face reflects just
so an eye catches its small
fluttery bright ache. How
much they count
on staying deeply
hidden from the living world. One,

a flash in a mirror. Another, smoke. Some count
time between city buses, others guess how
long it will be before he's deeply
homesick or she will sew
back the pearl shank button to its cuff: small
clocks the living run

on except when slipping deeply
into dead time: how like one
sweating afternoon, peeling small
bark strips off a stick until it's a tusk: how
like finding a note you can't
recall writing: how like the last of the soap

disappears. Origins of things no one
remembers clearly, this world so
closely resembling that part of purgatory. How
the dead who overloved forever count
fragrances of what they miss: beeswax, small
strawberries boiling to jam, chocolates in pleated

papers. They know how
fear of loss makes us susceptible,
suck kisses one by one
from letters: just as small
water beads on a mug are so
gracefully caught

by the lower lip. We follow the dead less certainly: the camp
road at night, how kids chase
after the flashlight's pool moving always slightly ahead.

Acknowledgements

With gratitude to my family, friends, and fellow writers, especially Nathaniel, Noah, Joe, Sharon, Coire, and the guys. Many thanks to my editor Barry Dempster for his guidance, skill, and dedication, and to Brick Books for its support throughout this process and its continued mission to publish Canadian voices. With appreciation for the work of Kitty Lewis, Alayna Munce, and Cheryl Dipede.

I have been privileged to attend the Banff Centre for the Arts, and have been influenced by the many talented people I met there. I especially want to thank Don McKay and Stephanie Bolster for their help with an earlier draft of this book.

I greatly appreciate the publishers and editors who housed some of these poems in their respective journals, including *The Fiddlehead*, *The Malahat Review*, *Prairie Fire*, *The Antigonish Review*, and *Smartish Pace*.

Lastly, this project spans many years, and I am thankful for knowing Lynne Tillman, Eric Keenaghan, Pierre Joris, Stephen North, James Lasdun, Katrine Raymond, Alice Zorn, Douglas Rothschild, Michael Peters, Jennifer Hill, Sam Truitt, Robert Ficociello, Leigh Kotsilidis, E. Alex Pierce, David Hickey, Travis Doyle, Judith Johnson, and my friends at the NYS Writers Institute. I'm indebted for your interventions, friendships, and conversation.

Charmaine Cadeau is the author of one previous collection of poetry, *What You Used to Wear* (Goose Lane, 2004). Born in Toronto, Ontario, she now lives in Winston-Salem, North Carolina, where she teaches and works as an editor. She holds a PhD in literature and writing.